Let's Draw!

2: Picture Squares

Colin Caket and Leon Baxter

Collins
in association with
Belitha Press

Let's draw together . . .

Drawing is fun so why not join in! This series of books will help you to put on paper the things you see around you, and the things you see in your head. There is no **right** way to draw — every artist has his or her own way of doing things. And so do you. These books will help you to find the way **you** like to draw, and give you some hints about what makes your picture 'work'.

I hope all the suggestions, ideas and games in **Let's Draw** will inspire you to create amazing pictures. Once you make a picture you like, you will be keen to draw more and more. Experiment! Use wax crayons and paint together — see what happens. Instead of colouring an area with just one coloured pencil, try two or more, or mix your pencil lines with areas of felt-tip colour. There are all sorts of things you can do.

Don't worry if your picture is not exactly how you want it to be — have another go. It's much better to do *lots* of practise drawings, than to attempt one precious masterpiece. But remember — don't waste paper, fill it to every corner and use both sides of your page.

If you **do** make lots of pictures your drawing will improve. Look at the pictures that you like and decide *why* you like them. Be encouraged by them and draw some more. Solving problems is easy and exciting.

Things you will need:

coloured pencils	paint
crayons	sticky coloured paper
pastels	lots of drawing paper
felt-tip pens	(white and coloured)

Have a good time!

Leon Baxter

First published 1988 by William Collins Sons and Co Ltd
in association with Belitha Press Limited,
31 Newington Green, London N16 9PU
Text and illustrations in this format copyright © Belitha Press 1988
Text and illustrations copyright © the estate of Colin Caket and Leon Baxter 1988
Art Director: Treld Bicknell   Editor: Carol Watson
ISBN 0 00 197707 5
Typesetting by Chambers Wallace, London
Printed in Italy

Heads, bodies and legs!

Trace over the squares below to sort out the funny people. This one is done for you.

Colour the squares below to look like these.

4

Now do the same here.

5

 Colour the squares below
like these . . .

and colour the squares
below like these.
Now finish the pictures.

Helpful squares

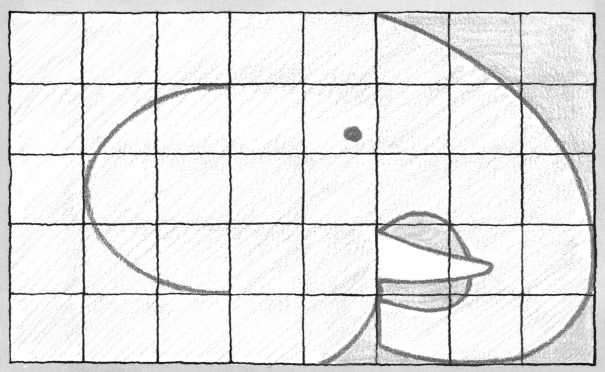

Can you make an elephant below?
Follow the squares.

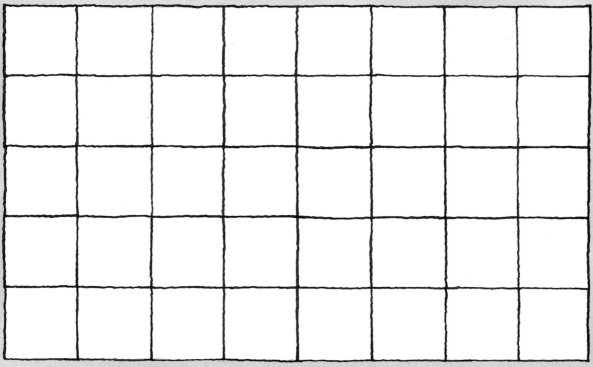

Now try a dinosaur.

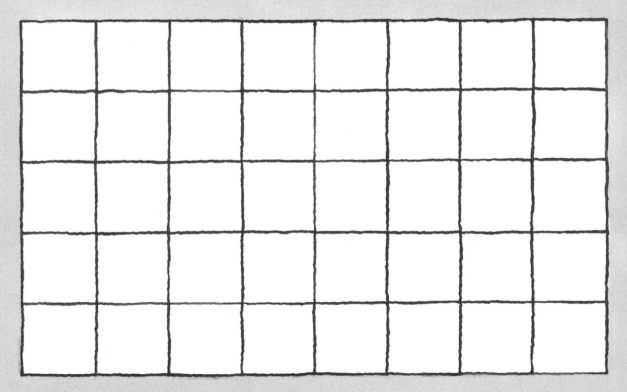

Each picture square shows part of the rabbit.

Can you use the squares below to
draw your own rabbit and colour it.

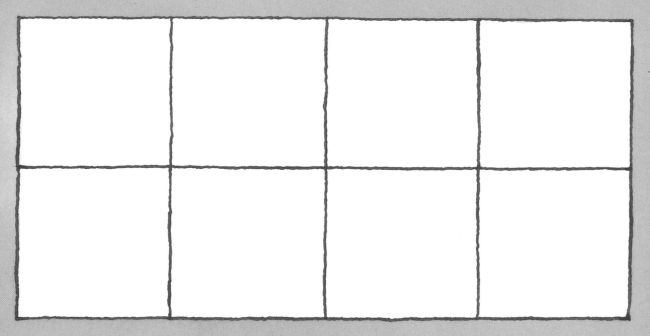

Can you draw this
running ostrich in
the two bottom squares.

The cross
will help
you to
begin.

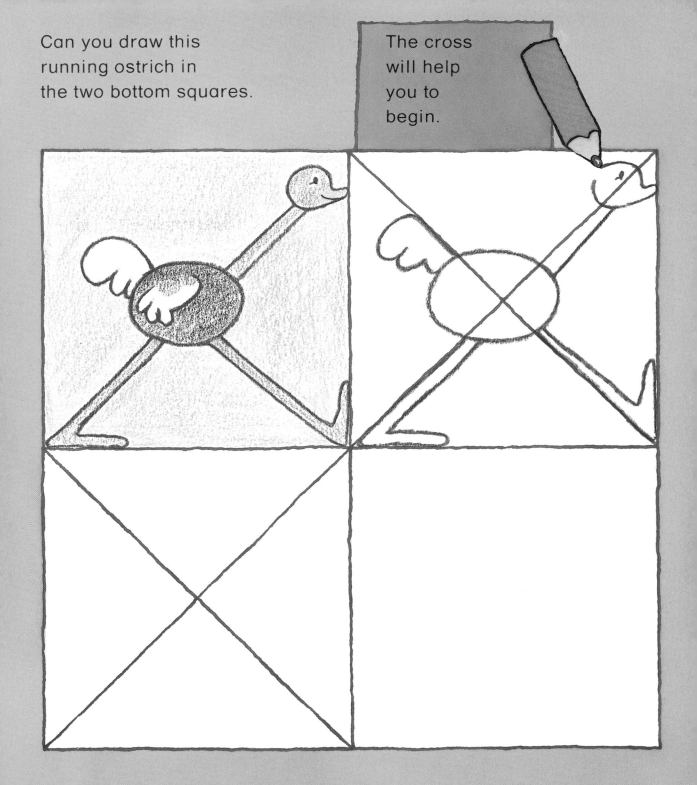

11

Make a house . . .

Use the squares below to help you draw this house.

Now colour it in.

and a boat.

Now see if you can use these squares to draw the boat.
But this time, make your picture bigger. I've made the squares larger to help you.

More useful squares:

too small

The elephant looks too small next to the mouse. Can you use the helpful squares below to make it larger?

14

too big

The mouse looks
too big next to
the elephant.
Can you use the
helpful squares to
make it smaller?

3 Now draw another car like this, but further away.

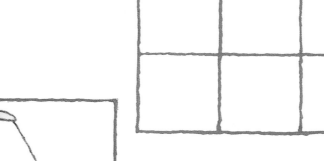

4 Now can you draw an ostrich which is closer to you than I am?

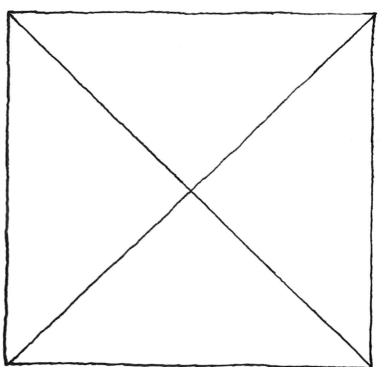

17

1 Here is a picture of a car.

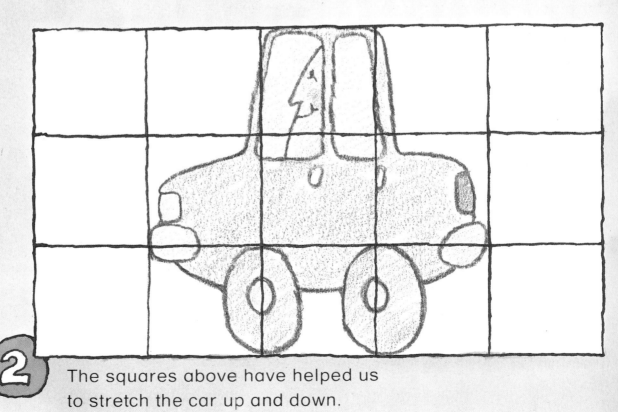

2 The squares above have helped us
to stretch the car up and down.

18

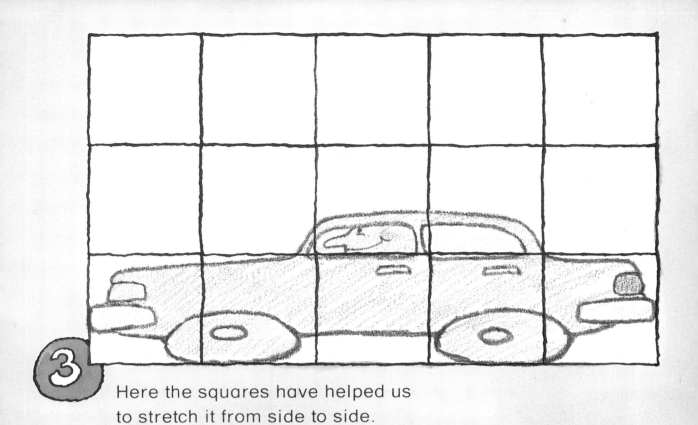

3 Here the squares have helped us to stretch it from side to side.

4 Now can you use the squares to draw the car the way *you* like it?

1 Here is a picture of an elephant.

2 Is this elephant too wide?

yes

no

3 Is this elephant too narrow?

☐ yes

☐ no

4 Now draw an elephant that *you* like.

Which of the other giraffes is too tall? Which is too short?

This giraffe is just the right size.

Now draw your own giraffe.

23

Can you help finish the view from the window?